HEROES
WHO HELP
US
From Around The World

Liz Gogerly
Ryan Wheatcroft

W
FRANKLIN WATTS
LONDON·SYDNEY

Franklin Watts

First published in Great Britain in
2019 by The Watts Publishing Group

Copyright © The Watts Publishing Group, 2019

Editor: Amy Pimperton
Design: Little Red Ant

HB ISBN: 978 1 4451 6567 7
PB ISBN: 978 1 4451 6568 4

Printed in China

Franklin Watts
An imprint of
Hachette Children's Group
Part of The Watts Publishing Group
Carmelite House
50 Victoria Embankment
London EC4Y ODZ

An Hachette UK Company

www.hachette.co.uk
www.franklinwatts.co.uk

FSC
www.fsc.org
MIX
Paper from
responsible sources
FSC® C104740

CONTENTS

HERE TO HELP!

What is a hero? Is it a brave person who risks their life to save others? Or is it someone that simply helps other people?

Heroes come in all shapes and sizes. 'Superheroes', such as firefighters, rush into burning buildings to rescue people.

Librarians are 'everyday' heroes who help people to find great books to read.

This guide dog is an animal hero. She helps her blind owner to move about safely.

Around the world, people and animals do jobs that help people. Other people become heroes simply by being kind.

DOCTORS

Doctors help us when we feel ill or if we are in pain. There are different kinds of doctors, such as general practitioners (GPs) and surgeons. Doctors are heroes of health!

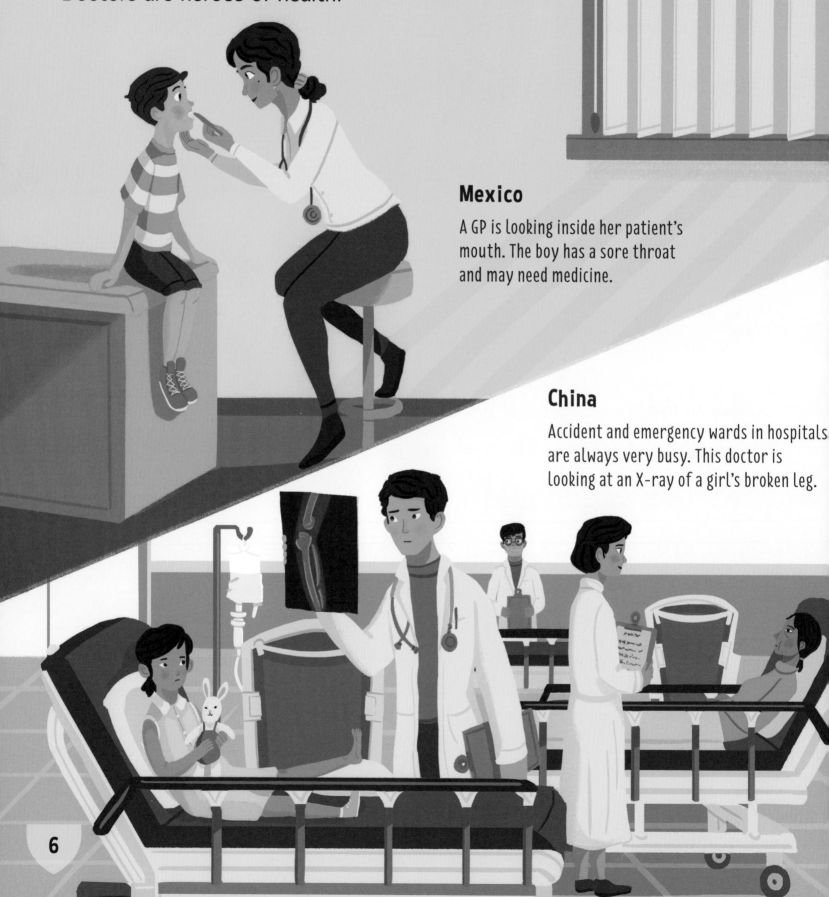

Mexico

A GP is looking inside her patient's mouth. The boy has a sore throat and may need medicine.

China

Accident and emergency wards in hospitals are always very busy. This doctor is looking at an X-ray of a girl's broken leg.

Ghana

This is a paediatric (children's) doctor. She makes the baby smile while she listens to his lungs.

Slovenia

Surgeons are doctors that perform operations. They save lots of lives!

Canada

In remote places, some doctors use mobile clinics to visit patients.

NURSES

Nurses work closely with doctors to care for and reassure us when we are ill. Injections and some health checks, such as blood tests, are done by nurses.

India

It is this nurse's job to weigh her patients and check their blood pressure.

USA

This friendly nurse is giving a child a vaccine injection.

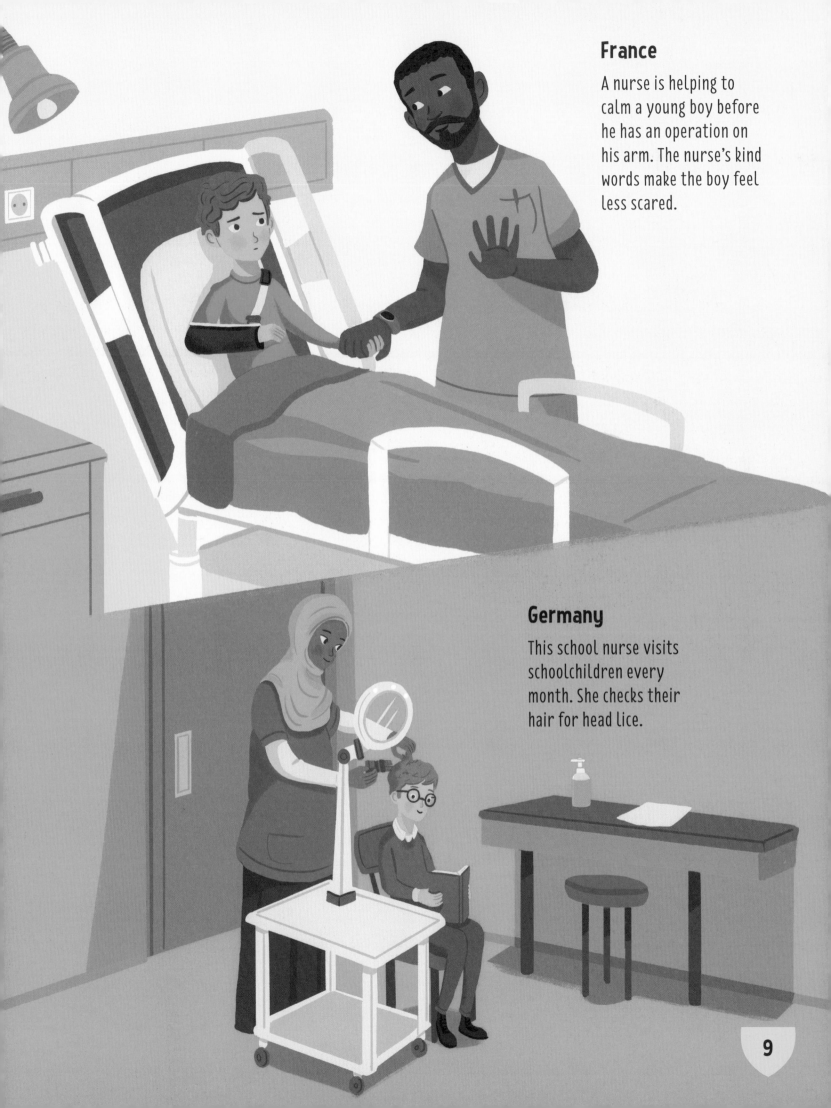

France

A nurse is helping to calm a young boy before he has an operation on his arm. The nurse's kind words make the boy feel less scared.

Germany

This school nurse visits schoolchildren every month. She checks their hair for head lice.

PARAMEDICS

An ambulance's sirens and flashing lights show that paramedics are on the move! They take people to hospital who have been in accidents or are suddenly taken ill. These heroes save many lives.

UK

Paramedics are often first at the scene of an accident. These paramedics are helping an injured motorcyclist.

Japan

Paramedics are taking a very sick man to hospital at high speed!

South Africa

Sometimes babies arrive before they reach a hospital. Paramedics delivered this new baby in the back of an ambulance.

Australia

Paramedics don't always use ambulances. Helicopters take paramedics to emergencies in hard-to-reach places.

Italy

Venice, in Italy, is built on lots of islands. Paramedics here use boats to get to emergencies quickly.

DENTISTS AND OPTICIANS

It is important to look after your teeth and eyes. Dentists help us to take care of our teeth. They look out for tooth decay and fix broken teeth. Opticians use eye tests to find out if people need glasses.

New Zealand

This patient's teeth are fine, but the dentist shows her how to clean her teeth properly.

Greece

Some people are scared to go to the dentist. This dentist is very friendly, which helps to calm his patients.

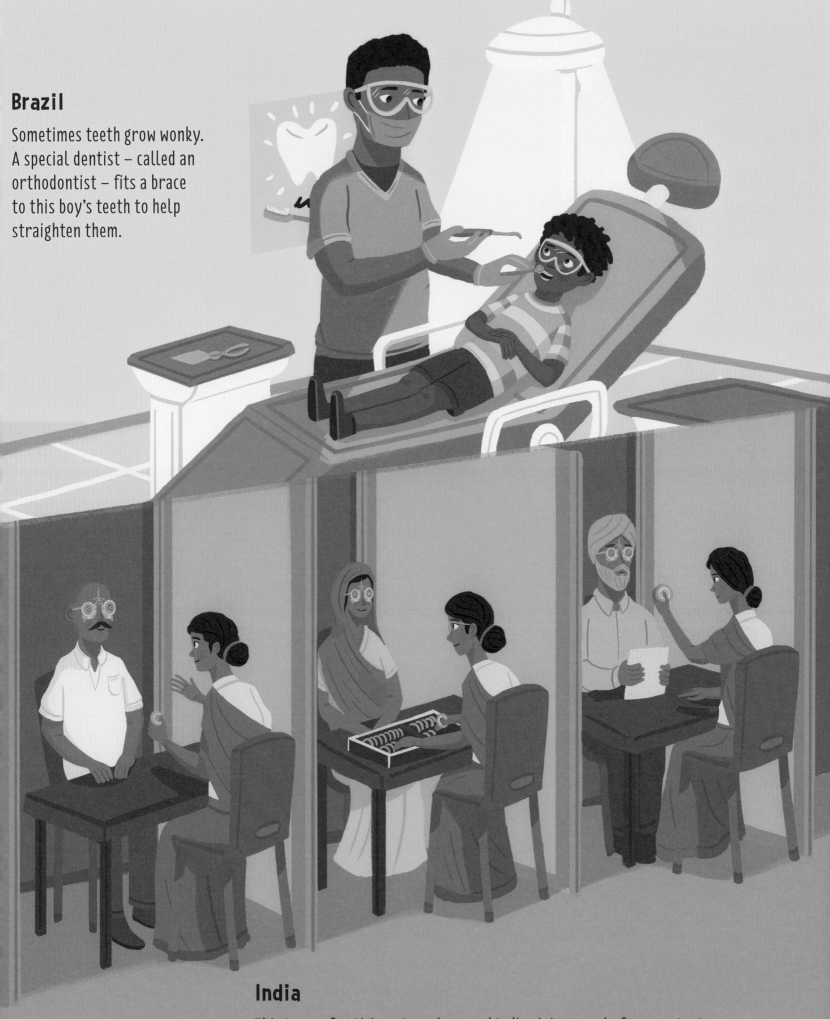

Brazil

Sometimes teeth grow wonky. A special dentist – called an orthodontist – fits a brace to this boy's teeth to help straighten them.

India

This team of opticians travel around India giving people free eye tests.

13

MIDWIVES

Around the world, about 350,000 babies are born each day. Many babies are delivered with a midwife's help. These heroes help mothers through the pregnancy and birth. Midwives also give advice on how to care for a new baby.

USA

A midwife checks that an unborn baby is growing well. He measures the bump to see how big the baby is.

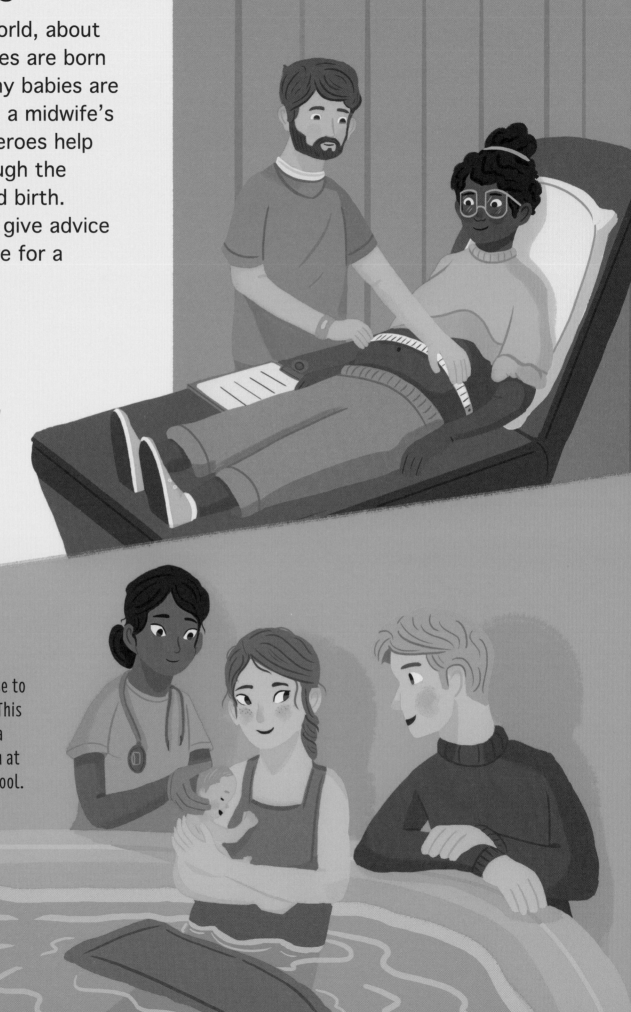

Denmark

Some mothers choose to give birth at home. This midwife has helped a mother to give birth at home in a birthing pool.

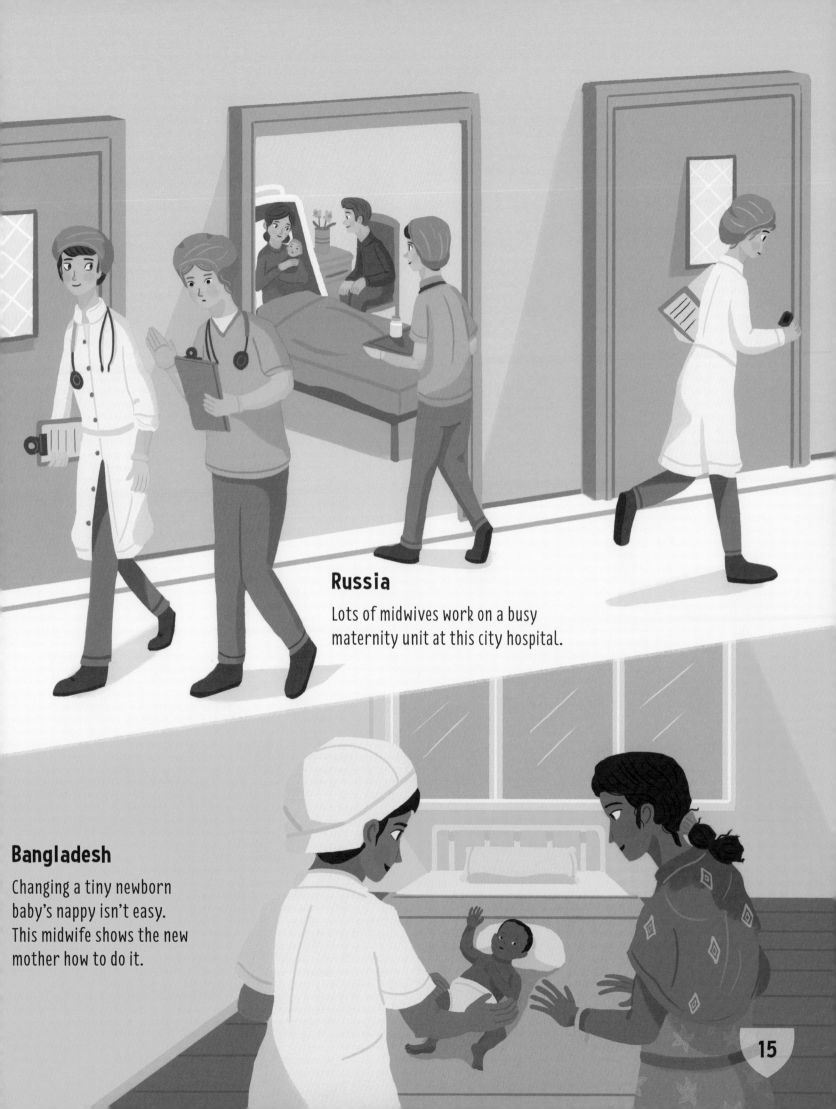

Russia

Lots of midwives work on a busy maternity unit at this city hospital.

Bangladesh

Changing a tiny newborn baby's nappy isn't easy. This midwife shows the new mother how to do it.

VETS

Animals need heroes, too. Vets (veterinary surgeons) treat ill and injured creatures, such as pet dogs, cats and rabbits. Some vets are experts in one type of animal, such as snakes or horses.

Canada

The animals in this busy waiting room all have an appointment to see a vet.

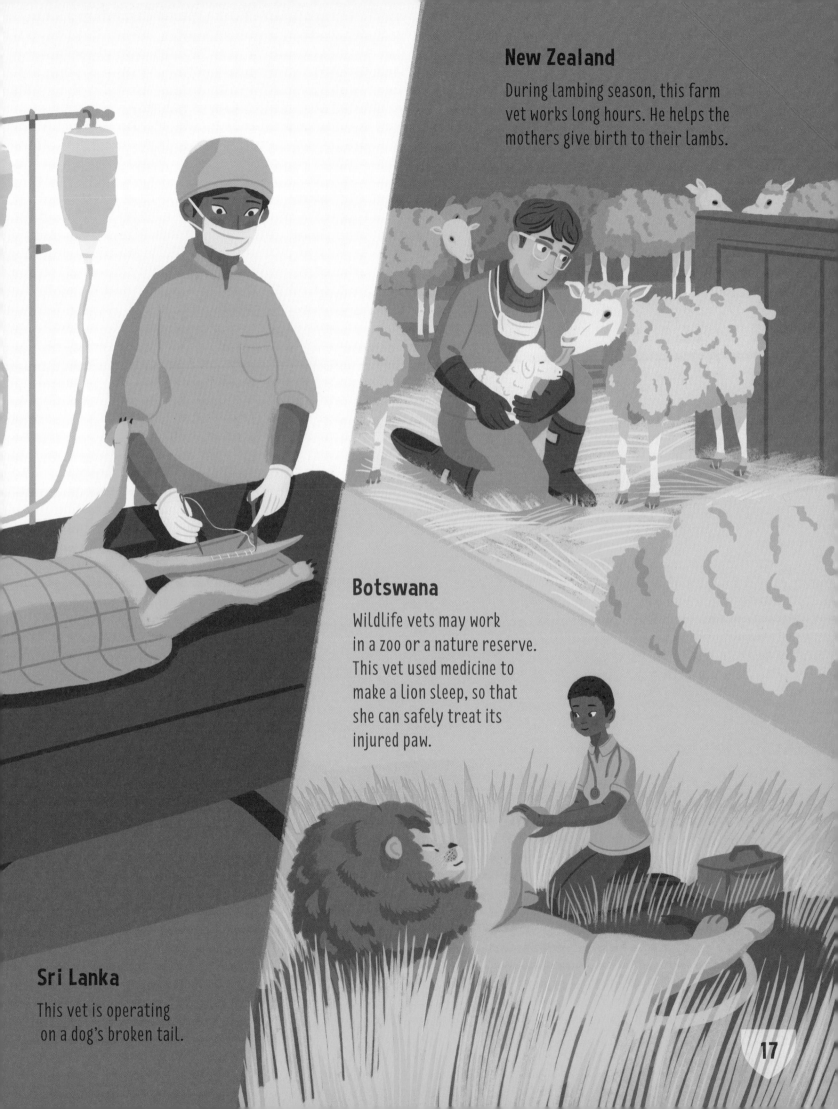

New Zealand

During lambing season, this farm vet works long hours. He helps the mothers give birth to their lambs.

Botswana

Wildlife vets may work in a zoo or a nature reserve. This vet used medicine to make a lion sleep, so that she can safely treat its injured paw.

Sri Lanka

This vet is operating on a dog's broken tail.

17

POLICE

The police are heroes who keep us safe. They solve crimes and make sure everyone obeys the law. The police are people we can trust if we are lost or are in danger.

Norway

Police officers on patrol help people to feel protected. Police patrol by foot, bike, car and even on horses.

USA

Police cars are easy to see and hear with their flashing lights and noisy sirens. A police car rushes to the scene of a crime at top speed!

Poland

These police officers are visiting a school to teach pupils about road safety.

Chile

Sometimes police work is dangerous. These officers are wearing body armour and helmets to protect themselves.

19

PARK RANGERS

All around the world, park rangers work in natural habitats, such as mountains and forests. They look after the land and the plants and animals that live there. These nature heroes also protect and conserve rare wildlife and habitats.

UK

This park ranger checks that pet dogs are kept on leads.

Kenya

A forest ranger plants trees to help conserve the forest.

Peru

This ranger conserves the rainforest to protect the rare hummingbirds that live there. He gets about by boat.

USA

In Yellowstone National Park, the rangers teach visitors about a geyser called 'Old Faithful'.

Russia

These park rangers protect tigers from poachers.

21

FIREFIGHTERS

Firefighters do a dangerous job. These superheroes really do rescue people from burning buildings. Firefighters also save people and animals from other dangerous situations.

Portugal

Firefighters face scorching fire, poisonous smoke and nasty gases. These firefighters are tackling a raging forest fire.

Spain

Firefighters are often on the scene of road crashes. They use special equipment to help free people trapped in cars.

Japan

Fires in big cities can spread quickly from building to building. Firefighters use hoses to put out the flames.

USA

This firefighter has rescued a cat from a tree!

Bangladesh

Firefighters help when there is a flash flood. Boats are used to rescue people.

23

MOUNTAIN RESCUE

Mountains are dangerous places where climbers and skiers can get lost or injured. It is very cold high up, with ice, snowy blizzards and even avalanches. Brave mountain rescue teams are the heroes here.

Nepal

Mount Everest is the tallest mountain in the world. This mountain rescue team use helicopters to rescue injured climbers.

South Africa

Thick, cold mist on top of Table Mountain makes things hard to see. It makes this rescue team's job very dangerous!

France

In the Alps, skiers sometimes get lost or trapped in avalanches. Mountain rescue workers carry radios, snow shovels and medical kits. Sometimes they have rescue dogs, too!

UK

This volunteer rescue team uses powerful vehicles to drive over rough ground.

25

TEACHERS

Teachers are heroes! The best teachers make learning fun. Great teachers inspire their pupils to be the best that they can be in life.

Italy

This teacher is talking to his students about writing stories. The children are excited to write stories of their own.

Pakistan

These children study outside in good weather. Their teacher knows that a hot classroom makes learning much harder!

Vietnam

This maths teacher works hard to teach her pupils. They enjoy her maths classes!

New Zealand

These adult pupils are being taught sign language by their teacher.

South Korea

These boys have a home tutor to help them learn more about lots of subjects.

LIBRARIANS

Books are important. People use them to learn and to read for fun. People that love books make great librarians. A librarian helps people borrow books, films and music from a library.

Nigeria

This librarian is using a computer to help find a book.

UK

The British Library is one of the biggest libraries in the world. The librarians here look after over 14 million books!

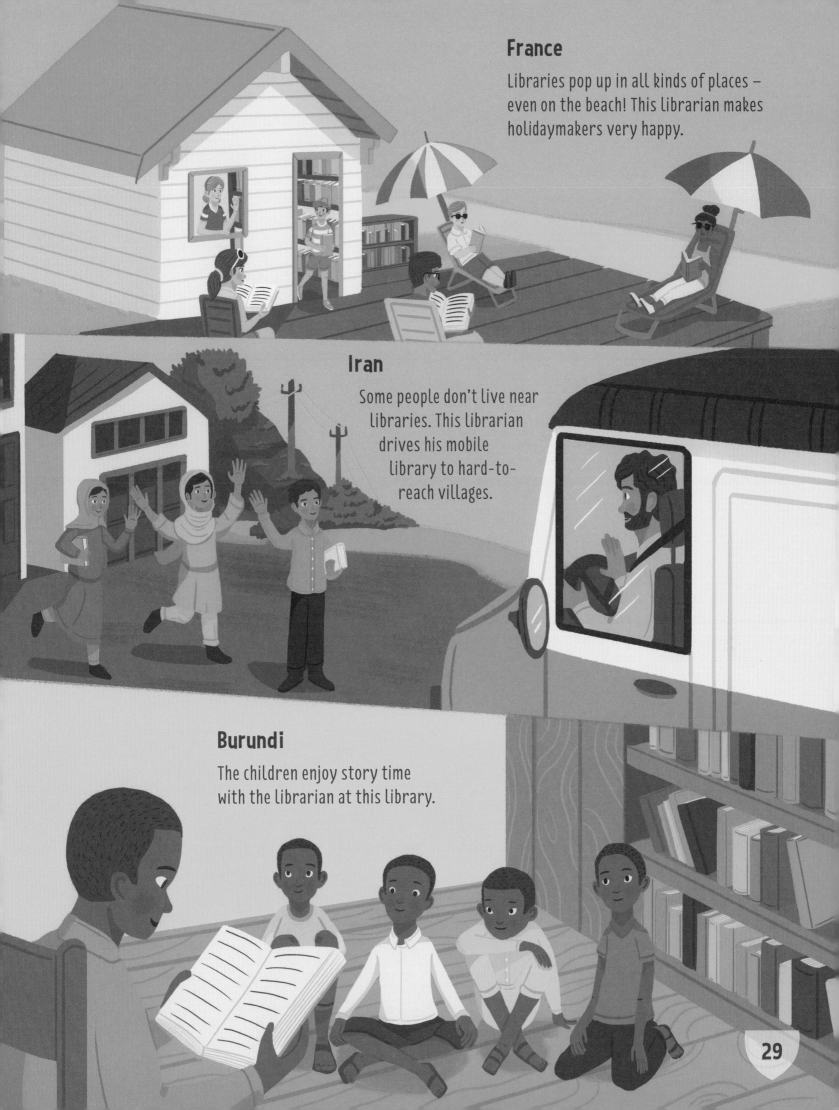

France

Libraries pop up in all kinds of places – even on the beach! This librarian makes holidaymakers very happy.

Iran

Some people don't live near libraries. This librarian drives his mobile library to hard-to-reach villages.

Burundi

The children enjoy story time with the librarian at this library.

29

NURSERY WORKERS AND CARE WORKERS

The very young and very old need heroes, too. Some young children may be looked after by nursery workers. The elderly may be looked after by family or nurses. Some old people live in care homes where care workers help them.

Thailand

This nursery worker sings a quiet lullaby to these young children to help them sleep.

Sweden

This nursery worker plays games with the children to make learning fun.

Republic of Ireland

Nurses and care workers help these old people stay well and happy. This care worker enjoys playing chess with a resident.

China

Some families look after their older relatives at home. This elderly grandfather is never lonely!

HELP AT HOME

Sometimes we might need people to come to our rescue in the home. All around the world, people rely on these everyday heroes.

Australia

Water is pouring all over this bathroom floor! A plumber has the right tools to fix the leak.

Jordan

This woman is happy that a plumber can fix her dripping taps.

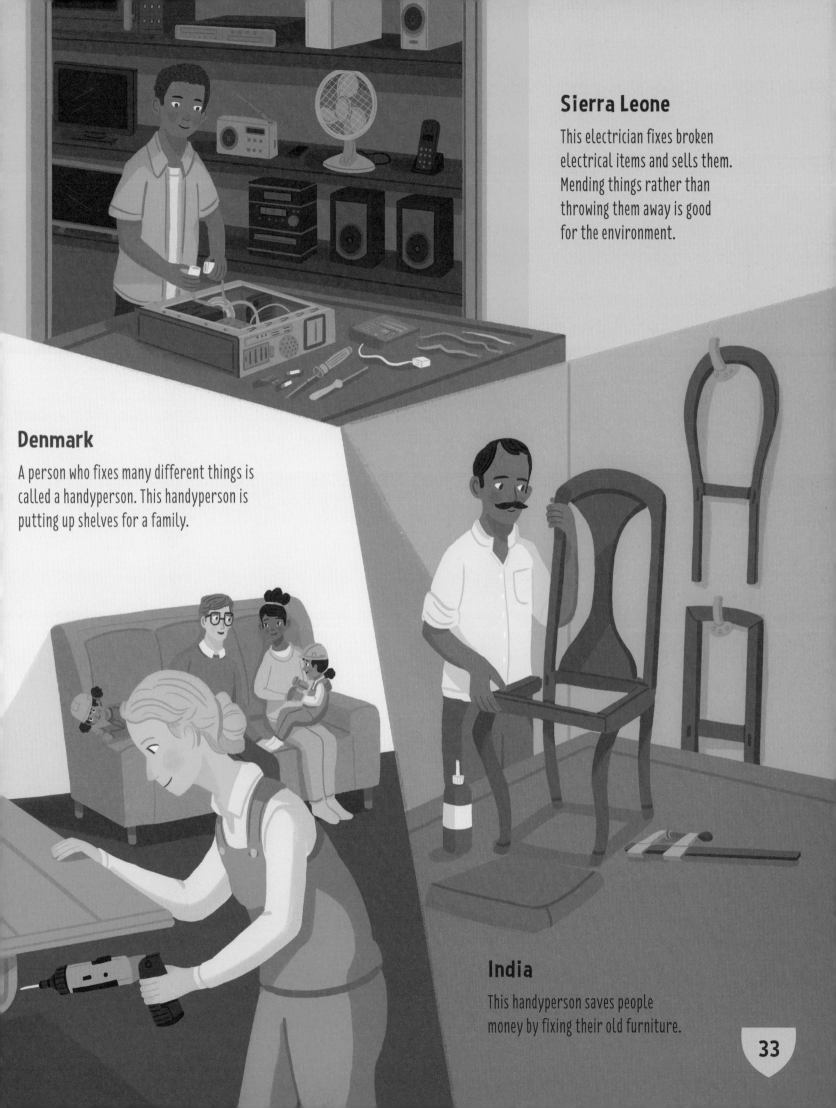

Sierra Leone

This electrician fixes broken electrical items and sells them. Mending things rather than throwing them away is good for the environment.

Denmark

A person who fixes many different things is called a handyperson. This handyperson is putting up shelves for a family.

India

This handyperson saves people money by fixing their old furniture.

33

OUT AND ABOUT

Some heroes are hard at work making our lives easier and safer. Postal workers deliver letters and parcels. Refuse workers collect rubbish and road safety officers help us to cross busy roads.

Germany

Postal workers get up early to deliver the mail. This postman makes his deliveries on a bright yellow bike.

USA

This postwoman uses a boat to deliver the mail. All the homes she delivers to are along a river.

UK

This friendly 'lollipop lady' helps schoolchildren cross busy roads. Her sign looks like a big lollipop!

Turkey

These refuse workers are heroes that do a very important job. They collect lots of rubbish in their big refuse truck.

SEA RESCUE

Hearing the words "mayday, mayday!" from a ship's radio means that people at sea are in danger. Sea rescue heroes are ready for emergency action in boats and helicopters.

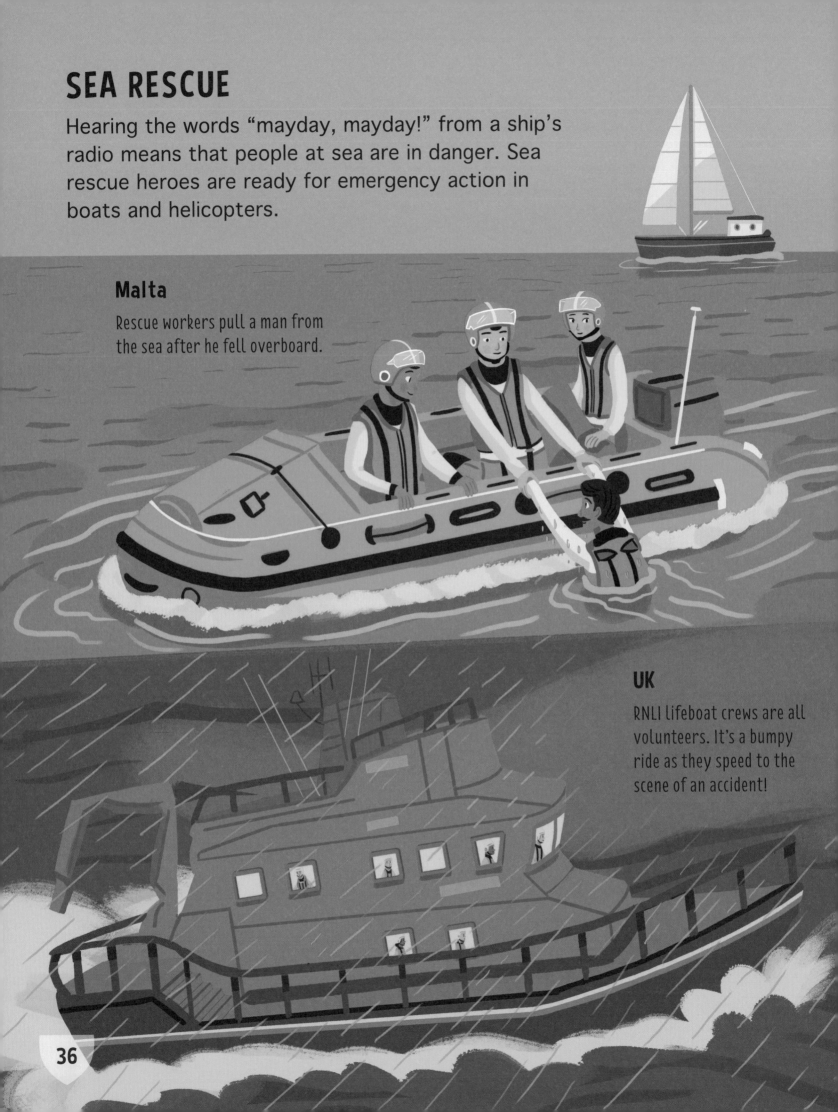

Malta

Rescue workers pull a man from the sea after he fell overboard.

UK

RNLI lifeboat crews are all volunteers. It's a bumpy ride as they speed to the scene of an accident!

USA

Sometimes the only way to reach a boat in trouble is by air. The US Coast Guard makes a heroic rescue with a helicopter.

Venezuela

Small tugboats are very strong for their size. This tugboat pilot is towing a stranded ship back to port.

LIFEGUARDS

Lifeguards help swimmers, surfers or people doing other water sports. They work at the beach, at swimming pools or near rivers and lakes. These strong swimmers act quickly to save lives.

The Bahamas

This lifeguard sits on a tall seat at the beach. From here he can spot sharks or people in trouble in the water.

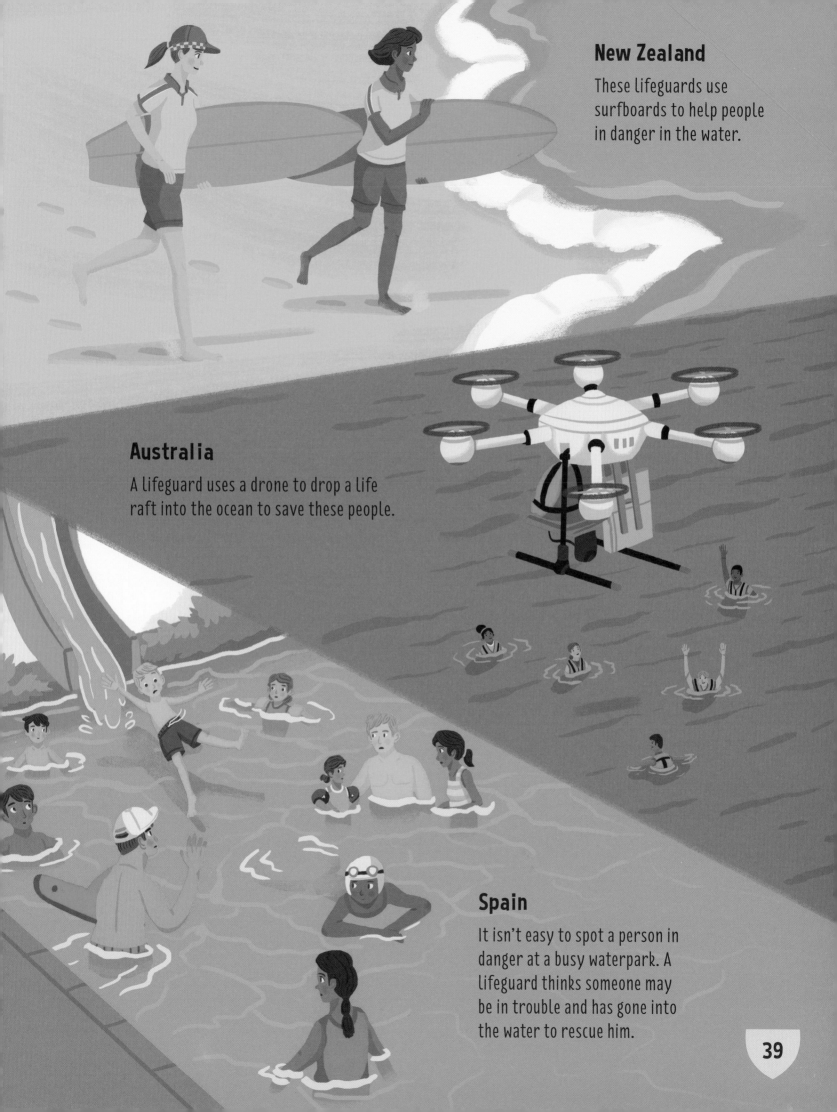

New Zealand

These lifeguards use surfboards to help people in danger in the water.

Australia

A lifeguard uses a drone to drop a life raft into the ocean to save these people.

Spain

It isn't easy to spot a person in danger at a busy waterpark. A lifeguard thinks someone may be in trouble and has gone into the water to rescue him.

39

VOLUNTEERS

People who volunteer their help don't get paid. Some of these everyday heroes volunteer in their local communities and some volunteer overseas.

Canada

Homeless people are often hungry and cold. These volunteers are giving them hot food and blankets.

Netherlands

These young people have volunteered to take two elderly women out for the day.

Germany

Conservation is important work. These volunteers enjoy helping out by planting trees.

India

Scout and Guide groups are led by volunteers. These Scouts are having a great day out with their leader.

Borneo

Orangutans are apes that are in danger of becoming extinct. Volunteer vets check the health of orangutans.

ANIMAL HEROES

All kinds of animals are helpful heroes. Dogs and horses can help disabled people or people who are unwell. Even elephants have rescued people from danger! Animals are heroes in lots of other ways, too!

Finland

This boy loves his hearing dog. She listens out for danger and is trained to wake him up if a fire alarm goes off at night.

Ecuador

These calm, cuddly ponies help unwell and disabled children learn to ride.

Qatar

These beautiful horses are working. Their police riders get a good view as they patrol the city.

China

Bees are heroes that pollinate flowers and make honey. Bees make more honey in China than anywhere else in the world.

43

Be A Hero, Too!

You may think that only adults can be heroes. Children make amazing heroes, too. You can be a hero in so many ways!

Here are some fun activities that will make you a hero!

Helping others

Helping other people makes their life better and it makes you feel good, too. Little things you do can make you a hero in someone else's eyes.

Walking an elderly neighbour's dog, helping them while they are out and about or offering to help tidy their garden can be very rewarding.

Organise a litter pick at your school or local park. Cleaning up the environment is a brilliant way to be a hero! Ask an adult to help you and wear gloves to protect your hands.

Helping out around the house can be fun. Try turning a chore into a game by seeing how fast you can do it – but make sure you do it well!

Be an eco hero!

Helping the planet is really important. What is good for the planet is good for everyone!

Bees help us by making tasty honey. Bees pollinate flowers as they collect pollen and nectar, which means that we can eat the delicious fruits and vegetables that plants produce.

Plant some colourful flowers at home or at school. This will help bumblebees and honeybees, who will drop by to collect the nectar and pollen.

Sharing

It feels good to share. You could start by sharing this book with a friend. Talk together about which jobs you think are the most heroic.

Baking cakes or other yummy food to sell at a charity bake sale can help others. The money raised can be used to buy useful or needed things.

You could give books, clothes or toys that you have outgrown to charity. They could make another child very happy. (Make sure you ask permission before you give anything away.)

As long as you help, share and care then you will always be a hero!

GLOSSARY

Alps a mountain range that crosses Austria, France, Italy and Switzerland

armour special clothing that protects the body

avalanche when a large amount of ice and snow falls down the side of a mountain

birthing pool an inflatable pool filled with warm water that a mother can give birth in

blizzard a large snowstorm with very strong winds

blood pressure a blood pressure test shows how well the heart pumps blood around the body

blood test where a small amount of blood is tested for diseases and other illnesses

brace wires fitted to the teeth to help straighten them

clinic a place where patients go to get medical help

conservation/conserve protecting the natural environment, such as by planting trees or helping endangered wildlife

elderly an old person

emergency a dangerous situation where help is needed quickly

expert a person who knows a lot about something or is very skilled at a particular job

extinct living things that have died out forever

flash flood a sudden flood of water, often after very heavy rain

forest fire a large fire in a forest or woodland

geyser a hole in the ground where boiling water and steam shoot up into the air from time-to-time

GP short for 'general practitioner'; a doctor in your local community who usually works in a medical centre

habitat the natural home of a plant or animal

head lice nits; small insects that live on human hair and feed on blood

injection where medicine is put into the body with a needle

law the rules of a country

maternity to do with pregnancy and the time shortly after a baby is born

nature reserve an area of land where the landscape, plants and animals are protected

nectar sugary liquid found inside flowers, which some animals like to eat

operation when doctors or vets mend parts of the body

overseas in a foreign country

patient a person receiving medical treatment, either from their GP or when in hospital

patrol to keep watch over an area, usually by walking or by driving around it

poacher a person who illegally hunts and kills animals

pollinate   when pollen is moved from one flower to another the plant can then produce fruit, vegetables, nuts or grains

port   a place where ships load and unload their cargo

pregnancy   a person or animal who is pregnant is carrying a baby inside them that will be born at a later date

rainforest   a dense forest that has heavy rainfall, usually found in hot and wet (tropical) parts of the world

rare   a thing or animal where only a small number of them are left

remote   far away; in a place that is hard to reach

RNLI   the Royal National Lifeboat Institution; the voluntary organisation of lifeboats and crew around the UK

siren   a loud warning sound used by emergency vehicles

tooth decay   when a tooth rots

tutor   a private teacher who usually teaches one person or a small group of people

vaccine   a medicine used to protect the body from getting a particular disease

ward   a room in a hospital where patients are treated

water sports   sports performed on water, such as windsurfing or jet skiing

X-ray   a special photograph used by doctors to see inside the body

FURTHER INFORMATION

Books

Busy People (series), (QED, 2019)
Here to Help (series), (Franklin Watts, 2017)
Popcorn: People Who Help Us (series), (Wayland 2012)
What Do Grown-ups Do All Day? by Virginie Morgand (Wide Eyed Editions, 2016)
What Do People Do All Day? by Richard Scarry (HarperCollins, 2018)

Websites

Take the quiz on this website to see what job might suit you the best.
www.kidzworld.com/quiz/2815-quiz-whats-your-job-personality/

The New South Wales fire and rescue website has a section that is packed with lots of fun activities and games.
www.brigadekids.com.au/

INDEX